Transitions Resource

RECOVER / DISCOVER IN GOD'S WORD

Transitions Resource

RECOVER / DISCOVER IN GOD'S WORD AGENDA

Session 1: Welcome and Introductions

The Benefits of a Structured Support Group

Court and Therapy/Support Groups are not the same

Pledge of Participation and Healing/ Participant Guidelines

Homework: My Personal Profile through Item 3 "Frightened and Scared"

Session 2: Grieving the Change-Frightened and Scared

Pledge

Open discussion of Item 3 only "Frightened and Scared"

Group exercise –Creative Visualization & Self Talk

Homework: Item 3 "Angry and Mad"

Session 3: Grieving the Change-Angry and Mad

Pledge

Open discussion of Item 3 "Angry and Mad"

Group exercise -Safe Techniques to Process Anger

Homework Item 3 "Sad or Depressed"

Session 4: Grieving the Change-Sad and Depressed

Pledge

Open discussion Item 3 "Sad or Depressed"

Group exercise-Putting Pain Away

Homework: Items 4-6 "Acceptance"

Session 5: Grieving the Change-Accepting Your Present

Pledge

Open discussion Items 4-6 "Acceptance"

Group exercise –Changing Your Story/Positive Affirmations

Homework: Item 7 "Hope and Joy"

Session 6: Grieving the Change-Hope and Joy

Pledge

Open discussion Item 7 "Hope and Joy"

Group exercise – Freedom of Forgiveness

Homework: Strengthen Your Faith

Session 7:   Strengthen Your Faith

     Pledge

     Open Discussion: Develop Your Faith, the Daily Prayer Habit

     Group Exercise: Group Prayer

     Homework: Be Grateful in Adversity

Session 8:   Be Grateful in Adversity

     Pledge

     Open Discussion: Living Gratefully Minded

     Group exercise-Daily Gratitude Journal

     Homework: Think Godly Thoughts

Session 9:   Think Godly Thoughts

     Pledge

     Open discussion: The Thought Habit, Choosing the Right Thoughts

     Group exercise –Turning a Wrong Thought into a Right Thought

     Homework: Speak Godly Words

Session 10:   Speak Godly Words

     Pledge

     Open discussion: The Word Habit, Speaking Blessings Daily

     Group exercise-Turning a Wrong Word into a Right Word

     Homework: Reduce Your Worry/Stress/Anxiety

Session 11:   Reduce Your Worry/Stress/Anxiety

     Pledge

     Open discussion: God's Design for Rest and Relaxation

     Group exercise-Christian Meditation through Prayer

     Homework: Discover Your Godly Purpose

Session 12:   Discover Your Godly Purpose

     Pledge

     Open discussion: Understand Your Value and Talents, Accepting Your Assignment

     Group exercise-Identify Your Purpose

     Homework: Live Your Godly Purpose

Session 13:   Live Your Godly Purpose

     Pledge

     Open discussion: How Servants Act, Living with Purpose

     Group exercise-Using What God Gave You

     Homework: Complete Your Plan of Action

RECOVER/DISCOVER

SESSION 1

Welcome and Introductions

The Benefits of a Structured Support Group

If you're facing a major stressful life change, you don't have to go it alone. A support group can help.

Support groups bring together people facing similar issues, whether that's illness, relationship problems or major life changes. Members of support groups often share experiences and advice. It can be helpful just getting to talk with other people who are in the same boat.

While not everyone wants or needs support beyond that offered by family and friends, you may find it helpful to turn to others outside your immediate circle. A support group can help you cope better and feel less isolated as you make connections with others facing similar challenges. A support group shouldn't replace your standard medical care, but it can be a valuable resource to help you cope.

Members of a support group typically share their personal experiences and offer one another emotional comfort and moral support. They may also offer practical advice and tips to help you cope with your situation. Benefits of participating in support groups may include:

- Feeling less lonely, isolated or judged

- Gaining a sense of empowerment and control

- Improving your coping skills and sense of adjustment

- Talking openly and honestly about your feelings

- Reducing distress, depression or anxiety

- Developing a clearer understanding of what to expect with your situation

- Getting practical advice or information about treatment options

- Comparing notes about resources, such as doctors and alternative options

Court and Therapy/Support Groups are NOT the same

The differences between what an Attorney versus Therapist/ Support Groups can provide:

   a. Court isn't for dirty laundry-Therapy/ Support Group is

   b. Court isn't healing- Therapy/Support Group is

   c. Court and the State law aren't necessarily fair

   d. Divorce isn't fair

Your Attorney is not your *Therapist, Doctor, Accountant, Buddy or Parent*, they are your *Legal Representative* only, can only help reach financial settlement/parenting plan.

Get what you need from the people that can provide it:

   a. Seek a **Therapist/Support Group** to process feelings, emotions, grief, expectations & rebuilding confidence

   b. Seek a **Doctor** for physical needs

   c. Maintain **Friendships** to keep you busy and occupied

   d. Use **Parents and Family** for unconditional support

   e. Hire an **Attorney** to legally dissolve a socially binding union and end marriage (Attorneys are not trained or equipped to help with emotional aspects)

Recover / Discover In God's Word Pledge

I pledge to acknowledge, validate and accept the wounding I have experienced.

I have the right and am entitled to these feelings.

I will take the time to grieve and mourn these feelings.

I will take time to study in group and on my own to develop my faith in understanding the purpose of these wounds and how it will help me grow and serve others.

I understand that clinging to negative thoughts and feelings only hinders my progress in processing my emotions.

I know that I owe myself the privilege to release these feelings and wounds in order to heal and become the hopeful and joyful person GOD says I deserve to be.

James 1:2-3 "Consider it pure joy whenever you face trials of many kinds because you know the testing of your faith develops perseverance".

Participant Guidelines

Confidentiality

This support group is designed to be a safe place to talk openly and share your challenges as well as your successes. It will remain a safe place only if the participants can trust that what is said in the group will not be shared with anyone outside the group.

Participation

While sharing your experience with the group is not required, most participants will experience more healing when they allow others to share their pain, grief and joys. This can only happen if everyone contributes to the group. The "homework" assignments are designed to be discussed at the following session, so completing the homework will be helpful in preparing your contribution and participation in the sessions.

Content of Participation

This structured program is designed to address the wounding and healing specifically related to divorce and your Ex-Spouse. While some participants may be in current relationships, please refrain from discussions of current relationships and share those experiences relating to your divorce, family and Ex-Spouse only.

Attendance

Participants are encouraged to make every effort to attend all of the sessions. The structured content is accumulative and is designed to work toward a healing outcome. Even if you feel the topic of a given week may not apply to you, your participation is a part of others healing and the entire group can gain from all experiences shared. We ask that you commit to attending as many sessions as possible.

Materials Needed

Participants need their own _Transitions Resource Recover/Discover in God's Word_ workbooks in order to personalize and journal their experience to gain the most benefit from the program. Participants can purchase the workbook on Create Space.com.

RECOVER/DISCOVER

SESSION 2

Grieving the Change-Frightened and Scared

MY PERSONAL PROFILE

1.   a. How long was my marriage_____

Minor Children Names/Ages_____

b. Any previous marriages_____

Related children to previous marriages_____

b. Where do I feel I am in the grieving process: (circle one)

Shock   Denial   Despair   Anger   Guilt   Bargaining   Acceptance   Forgiveness

c. How important is marriage or a partner to my self-concept (Scale 1-10)

10 very important   9   8   7   6   5   4   3   2   1 not important

d. What perceptions do I have regarding marriage in general? (my long term dreams of marriage)

1.

2.

3.

4.

5.

2.   a. I recollect most often the__ positive or__ negative aspects of marriage. Recollections:

1.

2.

3.

4.

My own contributions to the status of the marriage?

1.

2.

3.

3. Emotions: Fill in the blank for all that apply: ***Frightened or Scared:***

I feel
 rejected because_____

confused because_____

helpless because_____

powerless because_____

submissive because_____

insecure because_____

anxious because_____

embarrassed because_____

discouraged because_____

insignificant because_____

weak because_____

foolish because_____

Session 2 Group Exercise

Psalm 34:4 *"I sought the LORD, and he answered me; he delivered me from all my fears."*

Encouraging Quotes from God Calling:
p. 15 be not afraid, I will help you. God helps, God fights, God wins. You shall see. All is well.
p. 16 what cause have you to fear? Has He not cared for and protected you? Hope on. Hope gladly. Hope with certainty. Be calm, calm in My Power.
p. 51 just say "Jesus conquers, Jesus saves-every doubt-every evil-every fear, Jesus saves from fear"
p. 56 Have no fear. Fear is evil and perfect Love casts out fear. There is no room for fear in the heart in which I dwell. Fear destroys Hope. It cannot exist where Love and Faith is.
p. 65 I am here. Fear not. I am a God of Power. Just trust. I cannot and will not fail you. All is well. Courage.

When we feel frightened, scared or anxious, along with prayer and study of the word, self talk and creative visualization can also be tools to calm us and help us feel safe.

Creative Visualization:

Close your eyes and imagine in your mind a place that brings you comfort, warmth, safety and joy. For some this is a favorite vacation spot, a good memory of a childhood home, a special room or environment that one has visited that has brought them joy and peace. An example might be sitting in your favorite beach chair under a shaded umbrella, listening to the ocean roll in. An image that also comes to mind is sitting in the lap of Jesus or God, with his wings of protection enveloping you, a shield of protection surrounding you that cannot be penetrated by evil. Allow your senses to feel this place completely, feel the warmth of the sun, the breeze through your hair, smell the salty ocean air, see the tide gently rolling in and out in a calming rhythmic motion. Now add the calming self talk.

Self Talk:

Self talk is positive soothing words to speak to yourself either silently in your thoughts or out loud. Some examples would be:

"Everything is fine in the here and now, I am exactly where God wants me to be"

"I am safe, calm, relaxed, being held in the protective loving arms of God"

"God is with me, all is well"

As you visualize your safe place, repeat your preferred self-talk phrase over and over again until you have achieved a calm state.

RECOVER/DISCOVER

SESSION 3

Grieving the Change-Angry and Mad

Angry or Mad:

I feel:

hostile because_____

angry because_____

hateful because_____

critical because_____

jealous because_____

selfish because _____

frustrated because_____

furious because_____

irritated because _____

skeptical because_____

Session 3 Group Exercise

Proverbs
16:32 *Better a patient person than a warrior, one with self-control than one who takes a city.*
15:1 *A gentle answer turns away wrath, but a harsh word stirs up anger*
29:11 *Fools give full vent to their rage, but the wise bring calm in the end*

Encouraging quotes from God Calling
p.80 *Above all keep calm, unmoved. Go back into the silence to recover this calm when it is lost even for one moment, you can help nobody when you are agitated.*

Safe Techniques to Process Anger

Pent-up anger can cause a variety of emotional and physical problems if not expressed and processed properly. Anger is a normal emotion experienced during the grieving process of change. Here are some healthy, safe techniques to physically express your anger to bring unhealthy emotions to the surface, process and heal from your pain. Take the time each day or at least several times per week to use these techniques to process your anger and pain regardless if you don't feel angry. This will help you avoid damaging long-term physical symptoms of anger and help you heal more swiftly.

Wet Towel in the Tub

Take a large bath towel and *lightly* dampen it with water to give it weight (do not saturate it). Stand in a bathtub, holding the towel draped behind you with both hands on either end, bring the towel up over your head and down in front of your body, hitting the towel on the tub simultaneously grunting or yelling out loud OR you may express angry words…such as "why did you hurt me?", "I hate that __", "I am angry that ____".

Racquet on the Sofa

Take a sturdy racquet (tennis, racquetball) and pile sofa cushions/pillows on top of each other to a waist high height. Using the same method above, bring the racquet over your head and down onto the cushions simultaneously expressing your anger out loud.

Ice Cubes at a Tree

Take a tray of ice cubes outside and find a tree away from the house with a fairly large trunk. Stand several yards away from the tree and throw ice cubes one at a time at the tree expressing your anger out loud with each one.

These activities may result in tears, this is ok. Allow yourself to feel your anger and express your anger. Crying is a natural release for anger and pain, allow yourself the healing process of tears, you deserve to mourn and express your pain.

15

RECOVER/DISCOVER

SESSION 4

Grieving the Change-Sad and Depressed

Sad or Depressed:

I feel

sleepy because_____

bored because_____

lonely because_____

depressed because _____

ashamed because_____

guilty because_____

bashful because_____

stupid because_____

miserable because_____

inadequate because_____

inferior because_____

apathetic because_____

b. If I feel betrayed, then by whom? Partner   Self   God   Family   Friends   Employer

4. What is my level of acceptance about breakdown of relationship as I had planned, hoped, dreamed, expected?

Session 4 Group Exercise

Excerpt from Deceived-Claudia Black

"It is usually early in the recovery process that the pain seems overwhelming, but it will pass if you are willing to identify and own it. Feelings are transitory; they pass. As intense as your pain can be, trying to control and defend against your feelings prolongs the pain. Allow yourself to own them and be with them. A lot of what you are experiencing is the accumulation of many years of unacknowledged feelings related to loss and grief.

How long will it hurt? You will experience a wider range and greater depth of feelings as you feel safer. Your pain is both deep and wide. It lessens as you own your pain, shame and anger. You need to live with your pain, accept its' reality and practice healthy behavior until the hurt begins to ease. It may be helpful to think of grief as a hurricane-force wind. If you stand rigid and lock your knees, the wind will surely blow you over. Conversely if you stand and face the wind with balance and flexibility, leaning into it, you may sway like a palm tree, but you will find your strength and durability. Peace comes by walking *through* the pain, not around it. The process of grieving and attending to your losses will take months, and you will periodically find yourself back in the grief process when a specific issue is triggered-even years into your recovery journey. The depth and span of your suffering is strongly influenced by the degree of grief you allow yourself to experience in early recovery.

Freeing yourself from the mental frenzy. One of the biggest challenges grieving partners face is preoccupation and ruminating thoughts. Ruminating is a cognitive attempt to control the situation and to avoid the overwhelming emotions of the situation at a time when you are trying to make sense of it. This mental vigilance is a form of traumatizing yourself. You can be so consumed in your mind-set of preoccupation and rumination that it feels as if you are going crazy with the various images. To get out of your head requires a willingness to recognize that you are the one keeping yourself trapped in this mental frenzy. It begins by accepting that preoccupation doesn't help your situation and only keeps you trapped in defeated thinking."

Accept that you are powerless over other people, places and things but remember that you are NOT powerless over your actions in your recovery. In order to redirect your focus answer the following questions on slips of paper:

What thoughts/visions are the most painful to me?_____

In what ways do I try to control my ex partner?_____

What can I do about this right now to free myself?_____

What action can I take?_____

What decision can I make?_____

Place these slips of paper in a box, label the box "Worry Box" and put the box away in a closet or up on a shelf. Continue to add to the box any unhealthy ruminating thoughts that hinder your healing.

What does God say about Suffering?

James 1:2-3 *Consider it pure joy, my brothers and sisters, whenever you face trials of many kinds, because you know that the testing of your faith produces perseverance.*

Romans 8:18 *I consider that our present sufferings are not worth comparing with the glory that will be revealed in us*

1 Peter 4:12-19 *Dear friends, do not be surprised at the fiery ordeal that has come on you to test you, as though something strange were happening to you. But rejoice inasmuch as you participate in the sufferings of Christ, so that you may be overjoyed when his glory is revealed.*

1 Peter 1:6 *In all this you greatly rejoice, though now for a little while you may have had to suffer grief in all kinds of trials.*

1 Peter 5:10-11 *And the God of all grace, who called you to his eternal glory in Christ, after you have suffered a little while, will himself restore you and make you strong, firm and steadfast. To him be the power forever and ever.*

John 16:20 *Very truly I tell you, you will weep and mourn while the world rejoices. You will grieve, but your grief will turn to joy.*

Encouraging quotes from God Calling
p.214 *Remember that life's difficulties and troubles are not intended to arrest your progress, but to increase your speed. You must call new forces, new powers into action. Whatever it is must be surmounted, overcome, remember this. It is as a race. Nothing must daunt you. Do not let a difficulty conquer you. You must conquer it, my strength will be there awaiting you.*

RECOVER/DISCOVER

SESSION 5

Grieving the Change-Acceptance

Emotions. Fill in the blank for all that apply: *Acceptance*

I feel:

content because_____

 thoughtful because_____

intimate because_____

loving because_____

trusting because _____

nurturing because_____

pensive because_____

relaxed because_____

responsive because_____

serene because_____

sentimental because_____

thankful because_____

compassionate because _____

b. Define my idea of being fair and my Ex partner's idea of fair:

My idea:

My Ex Partner's idea:

c. Do I expect my Ex partner will be "fair" moving forward?

d. What do I predict to be the main areas of conflict regarding my Ex partner moving forward?

Specifically identify my value system by ranking the following items in order of importance:

Work, religion, family, extracurricular activities/hobbies

Specifically identify my Ex partner's value system in order of importance:

Identify similarities and differences and if I have violated my own value system in the events leading to divorce:

Current Life as I know it is ending, but it begins a new hopeful, improving, happy and healthier status than unhappily married. My current status of hope is:

10 very hopeful   9   8   7   6   5   4   3   2   1 hopeless

23

Session 5 Group Exercise

Motivational speaker Iyanla Vanzant recognizes that we can become addicted to our painful story of our past and encourages us to "get unstuck from our story" in 3 simple steps.

One: Look at how you contribute to your pain, tell yourself the TRUTH:
Who are you?
What do you want?
What are you willing to do to get it?
What are you not willing to do to get it?
State facts, speak the truth

Two: Ask for what you want. Be willing to get a "NO" answer but know how you will respond to this "no" answer

Three: Get a vision of what you want and put an action plan in place to achieve it

Example:
One:
I am a divorced widow, my children lost their father
I want to be a healthy role-model for my children, show them how to grieve and heal
I want to restore peace, love and joy to our home and environment
I am willing to seek Counseling for self and children
I am not willing to let this event make my children bitter, angry or unhealthy

Two:
Positive Affirmations: I am happy, healthy and joyful; my children are happy, healthy and joyful

Three:
We will tell jokes at the dinner table every night (make sure we laugh every day)
We will share stories daily of one thing that brought us joy that day
We will share a reading or anecdote daily that depicts hope/endurance through difficult times

Choose 5-10 verses, readings or positive affirmations, list them on a note card and read them daily. A list of sample verses and positive affirmations are on the following page.

Sample Verses

Proverbs 3:5-6 *Trust in the L*ORD *with all your heart and lean not on your own understanding; in all your ways submit to him, and he will make your paths straight.*

Sample Readings- God Calling

P. 14 *Be full of joy. Joy saves. Joy Cures. Joy in Me. In every ray of sunlight, every smile, every act of kindness, or love, every trifling service-joy. Refuse to be downcast.*

P.102 *Leave to Me the unraveling of the puzzles of life. Secure in the certainty that all that is wrong I can set right.*

P.112 *Breathe in the rich blessings of each new day-forget all that lies behind you. Man is so made that he can carry the weight of twenty-four hours-no more. I have promised to help you with the burden of today only, the past I have taken from you, and if you, foolish hearts choose to gather again that burden and bear it then indeed, you mock Me to expect Me to share it.*

P.164 *I say to you that you are not to dwell for one moment on the past. You must be as one who runs a race, stumbles and falls, rises and presses on to the goal. So with you, and I lay it on you as a command—no looking back. give yourself and all you have ever met a fresh start from today.*

Sample Positive Affirmations:

I am blessed with God's supernatural wisdom and have a clear direction for my life
I am blessed with Divine protection
I am blessed with self control and self discipline
I am the joyful being God wants me to be
I have the peace that God has assured me
God will see that I am victorious in all that I attempt
I have abundance and God showers me with blessings
I have an obedient heart and trust that the Lord will bare my burdens
I am loved and love others
I am forgiving and compassionate toward others
I trust in the Lord to right my wrongs and those who have wronged me
The more I give and serve the more I receive
I feel happy and blissful
I am kind, loving, courageous and have a great deal to share with others
All that is wrong the Lord will set right
I will focus on today and the blessings in store
I release my past to the Lord and focus on the blessings in store for me
I am happy, I am healthy, I am blessed
With God, all things are possible
The Lord is my healer

Acceptance

Acceptance is the final stage of grief and loss and is necessary to move through difficult feelings and situations into purposeful forward action. The other stages of grief are denial anger bargaining and sadness. In many situations people stay in the bargaining stage because the sadness seems overwhelming. Bargaining is trying to manipulate the situation to be what you want it to be or trying to make sense of it when there may be no sense to be made.

A good analogy of moving to acceptance is this scenario: If you woke up in the night and your kitchen was ABLAZE on fire, past the point of a bucket of water or fire extinguisher, what would you do? Certainly you would be grieving; grieving the idea of a good night's sleep, grieving the idea of safety in your home, grieving the loss of your kitchen and possibly your house. But if you were stuck in the bargaining stage you would stand on the edge of the fire saying things like, "Why is the kitchen on fire?", "The kitchen should NOT be on fire!", "If I were the kitchen I wouldn't be on fire!", "I am not moving from this spot until we figure out **WHY** the kitchen is on fire!". All of that sounds pretty ridiculous, doesn't it? To stand stagnant on the edge of a fire asking questions that don't change that the kitchen is indeed **ON FIRE.** If you didn't move from that spot you would burn up! Yet that's what we do in bargaining, we ask why and say how it should be rather than accepting that things are the way they are and all the why's and should's in the world won't change that.

Acceptance doesn't mean we are happy about the situation or that we are comfortable with it or that we don't try to change our involvement. It just means we accept that <u>it is what it is.</u> The kitchen is on fire, accept it, get out of the house, and call the fire dept. You cannot properly deal with a situation until you call it for what it is. If you are unsure of what it is, look at the history, track record, and probability. If you want your spouse to change, for example, look at their history of change and ask yourself how strong of a probability is it that this time will ACTUALLY be different? Ten percent? Twenty? Fifty? Five? You make the call on what's acceptable and how you will determine your boundaries. But remember, why's and should's will keep you stuck from moving forward. **Just get out of the kitchen!!**

RECOVER/DISCOVER

SESSION 6

Grieving the Change-Hope and Joy

Emotions: Fill in the blank to all that apply   *Hope:*

I feel:

proud because_____

respected because_____

appreciated because_____

hopeful because_____

important because_____

faithful because_____

cheerful because_____

satisfied because_____

valuable because_____

worthwhile because_____

intelligent because_____

confident because_____

forgiving because_____

Joy:

I feel:

excited because_____

daring because_____

energetic because_____

playful because_____

creative because_____

aware because_____

delightful because_____

extravagant because_____

amused because_____

stimulating because_____

fascinating because_____

28

Session 6 Group Exercise

Excerpt from **Deceived**-Claudia Black

"Forgiveness and recovery: The process of true forgiveness begins with acknowledging that a wrong has been done to you. Then you can grieve and own the feelings associated with those wrongs, your pain and anger. Even though the relationship is over, the act of forgiving is about your own healing; about letting go of resentments, preoccupations, and controlling behavior. Ultimately forgiveness is remembering and letting go. It is about being true to you and your higher self. Forgiveness is made possible with your commitment to your own recovery practices.

When you forgive, you no longer build an identity around something that happened to you. You realize that there is more to you than your history with your partner. You recognize that you no longer need your grudges, resentment, hatred or self-pity. You commit to changing your story for the present, the here and now. You don't need these negative emotions as excuses for getting less out of life than you want or deserve. You no longer want to punish the people who hurt you. Forgiveness is the inner peace you feel when you stop trying to do so."

Many people of faith choose to place the fate of those who hurt them in the hands of their higher power and free themselves from "righting the wrong" done to them. This allows them the ability to forgive, knowing that it is not their responsibility to settle the score.

Regarding faith as a means to survive devastatingly painful circumstances, Leslie Dinkins, LCSW, Domestic Violence Victim Counselor states "Of all the victims I have counseled, the majority of those who have emotionally survived and thrived are those that have a strong spiritual faith they rely on for hope and healing."

If not faith, those that rely on the old adage "Everything happens for a reason, and what am I supposed to learn and grow from this experience?" will identify their means to forgiveness.

"Forgiving is for ME, forgiving sets me FREE"

Today I will forgive _____ for _____

Today I will forgive _____ for _____

Today I will forgive _____ for _____

Today I will forgive _____ for _____

Today I will forgive _____ for _____

1 Peter 3:8-22 *Finally, all of you, be like-minded, be sympathetic, love one another, be compassionate and humble. Do not repay evil with evil or insult with insult. On the contrary, repay evil with blessing, because to this you were called so that you may inherit a blessing.*

Romans 5:1-4 *Therefore, since we have been justified through faith, we have peace with God through our Lord Jesus Christ, through whom we have gained access by faith into this grace in which we now stand. And we boast in the hope of the glory of God. Not only so, but we also glory in our sufferings, because we know that suffering produces perseverance; perseverance, character; and character, hope.*

1 Peter 1:6-7 *In all this you greatly rejoice, though now for a little while you may have had to suffer grief in all kinds of trials. These have come so that the proven genuineness of your faith—of greater worth than gold, which perishes even though refined by fire—may result in praise, glory and honor when Jesus Christ is revealed.*

1 Thessalonians 5:15-18 *Make sure that nobody pays back wrong for wrong, but always strive to do what is good for each other and for everyone else. Rejoice always, pray continually, give thanks in all circumstances; for this is God's will for you in Christ Jesus.*

Proverbs 12:20 *Deceit is in the hearts of those who plot evil, but those who promote peace have joy.*

Encouraging quotes from God Calling

p. 89 *Say often, "God Bless___" of any whom you find in disharmony with you, or whom you desire to help. Say it, willing that showers of blessings and joy and success may fall upon them. Leave to Me the necessary correcting or training; you must only desire joy and blessing for them. At present your prayers are that they should be taught and corrected. Oh! If My children would leave My work to Me and occupy themselves with the task I give them. Love, love, love. Love will break down all your difficulties. Love will build up all your successes. God the destroyer of evil, God the creator of good—is Love.*

p. 40 *You must rely on Me. Trust to the last uttermost limit. Trust and be not afraid. you must depend on Divine Power only. I have not forgotten you. Your help is coming. You shall know and realize My Power. Endurance is faith tried almost to breaking point. You must wait, and trust, and hope and joy in Me. You must not depend on man but on Me, your Strength, your Help, your Supply. You cannot be anxious if you know that I am your supply.*

p. 46 *You think that there is much to do in a crisis like this. There is only one thing to do. Link your lives on to the Divine Forces, and then, it is as much My work to see those lives and their affairs run in an orderly right manner as to see that tomorrow's Sun rises.*

p. 47 *How many of the world's prayers have gone unanswered because My children who prayed did not endure to the end. They thought it was too late, and that they must act for themselves, that I was not going to act for them. Remember My words: "He that endureth to the end, the same shall be saved." Can you endure to the end? If so, you shall be saved. But endure with courage, with Love and laughter.*

p. 81 *Perfect Love means perfect forgiveness.*
God is love, no judging
God is love, no resentment
God is love, all patience
God is love, all power
God is love, all supply

p. 106 *He brought me up also out of a horrible pit, out of the miry clay, and set my feet upon a rock and established my goings. Meditate upon that wonder-truth, the three steps—*
> *safety-He set my feet upon a rock*
> *security-He established my goings*
> *guidance-Is the final stage when the saved soul trusts me so entirely it seeks no more its own way but leave all future plans to Me its Rescuer*

p. 238 *Fullness of Joy. The Joy of Perpetual Guidance. The Joy in knowing that every detail of your lives is planned by Me, but planned with a wealth of tenderness and Love. Wait for guidance in every step. Wait to be shown My way.*

RECOVER/DISCOVER

SESSION 7

Strengthen Your Faith

Strengthen Your Faith

In *Making Good Habits*, Joyce Meyer states:

"Living by faith in God takes the pressure off of us and allows us to enjoy all of life in a greater way. Faith is God's will and should become our habit. Hebrews 11:16 says that without faith we cannot please God, Romans 14:23 says anything we do that is not done in faith is sin. Faith is trusting in what God says in His Word, even though you may not have any evidence of its reality yet."

God wants us to practice both *faith by evidence*, with work and miracles we have personally witnessed but more importantly *enduring faith,* sometimes called "blind faith". It is the enduring faith, the faith without proof, without question that allows one to place one's hope in HIS almighty power to work things out in your favor. Understand he hears your prayers, accept HIS timing to deliver your best possible outcome, honor Him with the enduring faith that gives you the ability to be positive in adversity and patient through the storm.

Proverbs 3:5 states *"Trust in the Lord with all your heart and lean not on your own understanding; in all your ways acknowledge him and he will make your paths straight."*

Meyer further states:

"I sometimes hear people say "I just don't have enough faith for that". But the truth is that we all have all the faith we need to do whatever God's will is for us. God has dealt to each one a measure of faith (Romans 12:3 NKJV). We all have faith, but the key to success is where we place it. If you put your faith in you or in other people, you will be disappointed, but if you put it in God, you will be amazed at what He can do through you."

Explain one personal experience where your faith was strengthened by acts, evidence, miracles that you have witnessed:

_____
_____
_____
_____
_____
_____

Explain one personal experience where your enduring, "blind" faith in hindsight resulted in your observance of a miracle or positive outcome you could never have anticipated:

_____
_____
_____
_____
_____

Develop the Prayer and Worship Habit

Meyer shares: "Take time first thing each day to communicate with your Father in heaven who loves you and wants to be involved in all that you do. You may not have a lot of time to spend with God in the morning, but to give Him no time at all is tragic and insulting. To seek him early in the morning is wise. Say to Him

"Good morning Lord, I love you. Thank You for everything You do for me. I need You. Please help me today."

OR

"In the morning You hear my voice O Lord; in the morning I prepare (a prayer, a sacrifice) for You and watch and wait (for You to speak to my heart). Psalm 5:3"

Listening to Christian music all day while in the car or at home can also be a regular form of worship.

OR

Read daily morning devotionals that quote scripture and include daily prayers (like _God Calling, Jesus Calling,). The Purpose Driven Life_ is a 30 day devotional. You can commit to reading one full Proverb per day or study Matthew 5 Beatitudes.

In _The Purpose Driven Life,_ Rick Warren says:

The heart of developing your faith is worship and the heart of worship is surrender. Surrendering to God is the heart of worship. It is the natural response to God's amazing love and mercy. We give ourselves to him, not out of fear or duty, but in love because he first loved us. However there are 3 barriers that block our total surrender to God, and they are _Fear, Pride and Confusion._

Fear keeps us from surrendering, but love casts our all fear. The more we realize how much God loves us, the easier the surrender becomes.

Pride keeps us from surrendering because we don't want to admit that we're just creatures and not in charge of everything, that we cannot control our fate. We still try to give orders and interfere with God's work within us.

Confusion keeps us from surrendering because we misunderstand the outcome of surrender. We relate surrender to being passive, a doormat, a coward, losing who we are.

The more we let God take us over, the more truly authentic selves we become, because He made us.

Signs that we know we have truly surrendered: we fully trust. We know we have fully surrendered (and developed our enduring faith) when we rely on God consistently to work things out instead of trying to manipulate others, force our own agenda and try to control the situation, we consistently let go and let God do his work.

Benefits of fully surrendering: we experience peace, freedom (a freedom felt like never before) and experience the miraculous power of God's will in our life.

Sometimes it takes years, but eventually we discover that the greatest hindrance to God's blessings in our lives is not others, but our own selves. Our self will, stubborn pride, personal ambition, own plans for ourselves that block God from doing His best work on us. So give it all to God: our past regrets, our present problems, our future ambitions, our fears, our dreams, our weaknesses, bad habits, hurts and hang-ups. Hand it over and put Him in the driver's seat and take our hands off the wheel."

List your personal blocks that are hindering God's work in your life:

Past regrets_____

Present problems_____

Fears_____

Weaknesses_____

Bad Habits_____

Hurts_____

Future Ambitions_____

Dreams_____

Now take the time to pray:

Pray for your enduring, blind faith to develop stronger, pray to release the specific items you listed above and turn them over into God's loving capable hands. Pray for God to show you ways you can further develop your prayer habits and faith development.

36

Session 7 Group Exercise

Pray every day, all day long and research God's word to overcome your pain.

Proverbs 2:1-15

My son, if you accept my words
  and store up my commands within you,
2 turning your ear to wisdom
  and applying your heart to understanding—
3 indeed, if you call out for insight
  and cry aloud for understanding,
4 and if you look for it as for silver
  and search for it as for hidden treasure,
5 then you will understand the fear of the LORD
  and find the knowledge of God.
6 For the LORD gives wisdom;
  from his mouth come knowledge and understanding.
7 He holds success in store for the upright,
  he is a shield to those whose walk is blameless,
8 for he guards the course of the just
  and protects the way of his faithful ones.

9 Then you will understand what is right and just
  and fair—every good path.
10 For wisdom will enter your heart,
  and knowledge will be pleasant to your soul.
11 Discretion will protect you,
  and understanding will guard you.

12 Wisdom will save you from the ways of wicked men,
  from men whose words are perverse,
13 who have left the straight paths
  to walk in dark ways,
14 who delight in doing wrong
  and rejoice in the perverseness of evil,
15 whose paths are crooked
  and who are devious in their ways

Share in a Group Prayer that focuses on asking God to help develop your enduring faith, establish daily prayer and worship habits, helps us to turn over all control to him and allows us to see the blessings he is bringing into our lives.

37

RECOVER/DISCOVER

SESSION 8

Be Grateful in Adversity

Be Grateful In Adversity

God wants us to be grateful for the good things, but also for the adversarial things that life throws at us. When you adjust your perspective to acknowledge and see the "silver lining around every dark cloud" you are developing your enduring faith in anticipation that there is a purpose, growth and a lesson in every experience that we have. In fact, God uses our challenges and suffering to test us, help us to develop our character and draw closer to him. The characteristics these adversities are intended to develop are: patience, courage, forgiveness, compassion, integrity and faith.

Rick Warren observes:

> "HE depends more on our circumstances to make us like Jesus than he depends on our reading the Bible. Jesus warned us that no one is immune to pain and suffering, that we would have problems in the world. Peter acknowledges that problems are normal and to be expected "*Don't be bewildered or surprised when you go through the fiery trials ahead, for this is not strange, unusual thing that is happening to you.*" 1 Peter 4:12

> *The Lord is close to the brokenhearted; he rescues those who are crushed in spirit.* Psalm 34:18 Your most profound and intimate experiences of worship will likely be in your darkest days-when your heart is broken, when you feel abandoned, when you are out of options, when the pain is the greatest-and you turn to God alone.

> Every problem is a character-building opportunity, and the more difficult it is, the greater the potential for building spiritual muscle and moral fiber. Paul said "*We know that these troubles produce patience, and patience produces character.*" Hebrews 5:8

> In these times of trouble, we need to continually remind ourselves that God's overall plan for us has yet to be revealed, but that his plan is good. The Bible tells us "*Give thanks in all circumstances, for this is God's will for you.*" 1 Thessalonians 5:18 *"Rejoice in the Lord Always"* Philippians 4:4"

James 1:2 encourages us to "*Consider it pure joy whenever you face trials of many kinds, because you know the testing of your faith develops perseverance.*"

Romans 8:28 encourages that "*All things will work together for your good.*"

While it may seem difficult in the height of crisis or heartache, God want us to have faith and acknowledge our blessings daily. If we cannot do this with the big things we are struggling with, we can at least start with the little things, something as simple as a pretty blue sky, the fact that we have our daily provisions; shelter over our heads, clothes on our back, food on our table.

The most powerful way to become gratefully-minded for our adversity is to acknowledge that God's timing is not always our timing. Accept that at some point God *will* reveal the blessings in store for what you have endured and that all of the suffering and heartache had a much bigger purpose and is a means to an end that we cannot see or even fathom at this time.

40

Take a personal inventory of your adversities, how you will expect to grow from them and acknowledge the blessings in your present circumstance.

Adversities and Challenges

1)_____

_____

2)_____

_____

3)_____

_____

4)_____

_____

5)_____

_____

6)_____

_____

7)_____

_____

8)_____

What characteristic will this help me develop

1)_____

_____

2)_____

_____

3)_____

_____

4)_____

_____

5)_____

_____

6)_____

_____

7)_____

_____

8)_____

I am blessed in the following areas because:

Family_____

Friends_____

Employment_____

Finances_____

Small daily observations of blessings_____

Monday_____

Tuesday_____

Wednesday_____

Thursday_____

Friday_____

Saturday_____

Sunday_____

<u>Session 8 Group Exercise</u>

Read the following scripture aloud together and have the group share their Adversities and Character building insights from the former exercise.

Patience:

Proverbs 19:11
A person's wisdom yields patience; it is to one's glory to overlook an offense.
Proverbs 15:18
A hot-tempered person stirs up conflict, but the one who is patient calms a quarrel.
Psalms 40:1-3
I waited patiently for the Lord*; he turned to me and heard my cry. He lifted me out of the slimy pit, out of the mud and mire; he set my feet on a rock and gave me a firm place to stand. He put a new song in my mouth, a hymn of praise to our God.*

Courage:

1Corinthians 16: 13
Be on your guard; stand firm in the faith; be courageous; be strong. Do everything in love.

Forgiveness:

Ephesians 4:32
Be kind and compassionate to one another, forgiving each other, just as in Christ God forgave you.

Compassion:

1 Peter 3:8
Finally, all of you, be like-minded, be sympathetic, love one another, be compassionate and humble.

Integrity:

Proverbs 10:9
Whoever walks in integrity walks securely, but whoever takes crooked paths will be found out.

Faith:

Proverbs 3:5-6
Trust in the Lord *with all your heart and lean not on your own understanding, in all your ways submit to him, and he will make your paths straight.*

Have the group share their Blessings journaling from homework and assign participants to get a small daily log (or hand out small bound pads or diaries to them) and commit to adding two items each day at the end of the day that they were grateful for.

RECOVER/DISCOVER

SESSION 9

Think Godly Thoughts

Think Godly Thoughts

We have already explored the benefits of Godly positive affirmations. Joyce Meyer explains:

"When you are trying to develop a good habit or break a bad one, always remember that thoughts precede words, words precede action. Or, as I frequently say, "Where the mind goes, the man follows." We must learn to think what we truly want, not what we feel, or even what we currently have. Start agreeing with God's Word that teaches us that all things are possible with God. Start purposely thinking "It is not God's will for me to be in emotional bondage, I am going to do all I can to get out. If I do what I can do, God will do what I cannot do." This may take a long time, but stick with it until you are free. Thinking like this will give you a mindset geared toward victory. It will change your attitude, your words as well as your actions. We can literally talk ourselves into victory or defeat. Don't ever settle for anything less that the best that God offers you. This is one of the main reasons we need the positive thought/positive word habit. In Matthew 9:29, Jesus told people that they would have what they believed, that they had to renew their minds to think like God thinks, so they could have the blessings that God wanted them to have.

Be warned! As you learn that you can change the things in your life that are unfruitful and causing you pain, the devil will offer you many excuses to stay the way you are. You may hear in your head "I can't help what I think, the thoughts just come whether I want them or not, without being invited". It is not true that you cannot do anything about them. In 2 Corinthians 10:5 God's Words teaches us to "cast down, or refute wrong thoughts." That means that we are not to allow them to stay in our mind. You can rid yourself of any unpleasant thought by simply deciding to think something else. Positive affirmations help in this process. Take responsibility for your thoughts and begin choosing them carefully because they are the raw material for your words and actions. The apostle Paul teaches us in Romans that God has a good plan, a perfect will for each of us, but we must renew our minds according to His Word if we want to prove it out in our experience."

"Be ye transformed by the renewing of your mind" Romans 12:2

In *The Anxiety Cure,* Dr. Archibald Hart explains that in order to change our thinking habits, first we have to "capture" our thoughts rushing through our mind before we can change them. He shares a 3 step strategy to changing our thinking habits:

"
      1) slow down your thinking
      2) challenge your mistaken beliefs
      3) speak the truth to yourself

Slow down your thinking and try to move them from a subconscious state to a conscious state, be aware of your thoughts rather than just letting them flow.

Challenge your mistaken beliefs by getting yourself a little notebook to record your beliefs whenever you catch them. Date the page. Throughout the day try to capture and record thoughts that imply beliefs that may be mistaken. Then write down your challenge of that mistaken belief. As an example:

Mistaken Belief: I am the victim of the way others have treated me.

Challenge: Nonsense, I can take control of my life now and change the outcome.

Mistaken Belief: People should always love and respect me.

Challenge: Who says? People respond to me in the way I treat them. If I want respect, I must show respect.

Mistaken Belief: I am just the way I am, I can't change.

Challenge: Not true, the gospel is all about change, it may not be easy but everyone can change.

Speak the truth to yourself by establishing a set of well-rehearsed self-statements you can draw on when you need to counter an unhealthy thought. These need to be rehearsed frequently so that they spring to mind when you need them, so write them down and take the time to memorize them. Here are some samples, but add some of your own that will be most effective for you:

I don't need to fight my feelings, they only last a short time, then they go away
I am going to focus my thoughts away from my hurtful feelings
So I feel some hurt (pain) right now, so what, everyone feels hurt (pain) some time or other
I am going to be alright in a short while, so I will think about something else and continue what I'm doing
Heartbreak (or pain) is as old as time, I don't have to allow it to control me, I can control it
Right now I am having feelings I don't like, but I know how to treat them so that they will go away
This seems like an impossible situation right now, but I won't feel helpless, I'll move forward with courage
I can control my feelings, I choose to overlook them and focus on other things
Feelings are only phantoms-they exist only if I allow them to"

<u>Session 9 Group Exercise</u>

Review Session 4 Healing Exercise "Free yourself from the mental frenzy" paragraph.

Proverbs 14:15
The simple believe anything, but the prudent give thought to their steps

List your top 5 Mistaken Beliefs

1)_____

2)_____

3)_____

4)_____

5)_____

List Your Challenges that correlate to your top 5 Mistaken Beliefs by number

1)_____

2)_____

3)_____

4)_____

5)_____

List your Top 5 Truths that you want to memorize

1)_____

2)_____

3)_____

4)_____

5)_____

Have each participant share their top 2 in each category.

RECOVER/DISCOVER

SESSION 10

Speak Godly Words

Speak Godly Words

We have studied how your thoughts can determine your words, your words can determine your actions. What you say out loud in the midst of your challenge has a lasting impact on how long you stay in those situations. Proverbs 13:3 states *"He who guards his lips guards his life, but he who speaks rashly will come to ruin"* and 18:21 states *"The tongue has the power of life and death, and those who love it will eat its fruit."* When you continually speak of how wronged you have been or how hurt and unhappy you are, you will continually remain in the downtrodden or victim mindset, however when you speak of how blessed, happy, joyful, healed you are, you are preparing yourself for the blessings God wants to deliver to you.

If it is too difficult to speak of your blessings just yet, then try to focus on speaking about your enduring faith that God has your fate in his hands and will redeem you. Job 25 is helpful with this "I will repay you for the years the locusts have eaten". Our faithfulness to the Lord will redeem our broken hearts. If we continually remind ourselves out loud and in our conversations that God will restore our health, and heal our wounds and broken hearts, we are giving roots to and sowing seeds for our actions.

A wise mentor once said *"God never commanded us to repeatedly verbalize our pain and suffering. He didn't instruct us to go around discussing our negative situations with all of our friends, neighbors and co-workers. Instead God told us to speak constantly of His goodness, his promises, his grace."*

Watch your thoughts, for they become words.
Watch your words, for they become actions.
Watch your actions, for they become habits.
Watch your habits, for they become character.
Watch your character, for it becomes your destiny.

Session 10 Group Exercise

Psalms 39:1

I said, "I will watch my ways and keep my tongue from sin; I will put a muzzle on my mouth while in the presence of the wicked

James 3:1-10

<u>*Taming the Tongue*</u>

Not many of you should become teachers, my fellow believers, because you know that we who teach will be judged more strictly. [2] We all stumble in many ways. Anyone who is never at fault in what they say is perfect, able to keep their whole body in check.

[3] When we put bits into the mouths of horses to make them obey us, we can turn the whole animal. [4] Or take ships as an example. Although they are so large and are driven by strong winds, they are steered by a very small rudder wherever the pilot wants to go. [5] Likewise, the tongue is a small part of the body, but it makes great boasts. Consider what a great forest is set on fire by a small spark. [6] The tongue also is a fire, a world of evil among the parts of the body. It corrupts the whole body, sets the whole course of one's life on fire, and is itself set on fire by hell.

[7] All kinds of animals, birds, reptiles and sea creatures are being tamed and have been tamed by mankind, [8] but no human being can tame the tongue. It is a restless evil, full of deadly poison.

[9] With the tongue we praise our Lord and Father, and with it we curse human beings, who have been made in God's likeness. [10] Out of the same mouth come praise and cursing. My brothers and sisters, this should not be.

Proverbs 12:25

Anxiety weighs down the heart, but a kind word cheers it up

Write 5 Godly Affirmations or positive, assuring Bible Verses on a 3 X 5 note card and commit to reading them daily or multiple times per day. Some individuals like to tape these to their bathroom mirrors so that they see them first thing in the morning, last thing in the evening. Have the group share their top 2 from their note cards.

RECOVER/DISCOVER

SESSION 11

Reduce Your Worry/Stress/Anxiety

Reduce Your Worry, Stress and Anxiety

In _The Anxiety Cure,_ Dr. Archibald Hart prescribes:

"Time for rest must be taken on a daily basis and should never be delayed longer than a week. In Exodus 23:12 the seventh day is noted as holy and for rest so that all may be refreshed. But the literal observance of the Sabbath is not what I am advocating here. It is the principle of a Sabbath that I think we need to observe. It is more than observing one day of rest. Every day needs its hours of rest (a good night's sleep for example). And every week needs its day of rest (for worship). Seven ways you can maintain the principle of a sabbath rest are:
1) Pay careful attention to developing an awareness of your limits.
2) Never work until you have reached your limits.
3) The moment you realize you are approaching your limits, stop.
4) Maintain regular breaks during your workday.
5) If you exceed your limits and find yourself in stress or pain, back off and allow time for recovery.
6) Take a good sabbath rest at the end of every day.
7) Take a good sabbath rest at weekends.

What is rest? Rest is not catching up on activities or participating in hobbies. What characterizes rest is that it is not an activity. It is pure, luxurious leisure, a time to rediscover yourself, catch up on your feelings, determine your new priorities, recreate a sense of balance, restore your soul and reconnect with God.

Resting is not the same as relaxing. We need to learn how to rest as well as relax. Relaxation involves turning off both your mind and your muscles. Relaxation lowers your stress hormones, including adrenaline and the "sad messengers" like cortisol. It elevates your immune system, raises your tolerance for pain, increases your natural tranquilizers, allows damaged tissue to repair itself and helps your body rejuvenate itself. So how does one relax? The basic ingredients in all relaxation include:
1) sit or lie in a comfortable position
2) ensure you won't be interrupted
3) set aside a predetermined amount of time for the exercise (30-45 minutes is ideal)
4) don't fall asleep
5) remain inactive (don't fidget, move, get up or scratch)
6) avoid thinking troublesome thoughts

One form of relaxation is Christian Meditation. The New Age's emphasis on meditation has put the fear of life into Christians many of whom have rejected the very idea as unchristian. This is a pity, New Age nor any eastern or religious system does not own meditation. We Christians need to rediscover the value of meditation by putting Christ at the center of it. Psalm 19:14 declares "_May the words of my mouth and the meditation of my heart be pleasing in your sight, O Lord, my Rock and my Redeemer._ Jesus Himself withdrew regularly from His disciples and the throng following Him to go into the hills and be alone with God. These were times of spiritual and physical refreshment after which He returned to His ministry with renewed energy and vigor. The very act of prayer, as the meeting with God, is a form of meditation. In concentrative meditation, a person seeks to restrict awareness of the outside world by focusing attention on an object or thought. Webster's Dictionary defines mediation as "_Deep reflection on sacred matters as a devotional act; study; ponder; to think deeply and continuously._" This definition guides us exactly into what Christian meditation is. So we Christians could do with a lot more deep reflection on matters to do with our faith and Christian experience. Therefore there are two essential ingredients you need to focus on as you develop your ability to practice Christian meditation. First-develop an ability to focus on something specific and second- get into the habit of worshiping beyond attendance at church. Here are five ways for meditation that I recommend:

Surrendering Your Will to God-Be deliberate in "letting go" or surrendering your life to God. Imagine that Jesus is standing in front of you, beckoning you to hand over all that bothers you. Be still; be quiet. Practice focusing on God. Imagine Him inviting you to hand over your tensions and worries.

Meditational Prayer-Periodically pray a meditational prayer that praises God and expresses your thankfulness to Him, then silence yourself. Invite God to speak to you. He will speak to you with thoughts, feelings and reminders.

Meditating on Scripture-Select a verse or two of Scripture you want to focus on. Read the passage in several translations until you understand its real meaning. Memorize the version you prefer, then put away the Bible and begin meditating each part of the verse. Try to discern what it is you believe God would like to say to you there and then about that verse.

Contemplate Who God Is-Ponder His love, grace and mercy for you. Try to recall portions or stories from Scripture that show God's love, grace and mercy. Read the story of the woman taken in adultery (John 8:2). Ponder God's compassion (Matthew 9:36, 15:32)

Experience God's Presence-Remind yourself that God is closer to you than you are to yourself, develop your awareness and sensitivity to His presence. Concentrate on God, try to find an image that helps you to imagine and visualize God, such as a shepherd, tending sheep as they lie down, fetching the stray lambs, leading them on to newer and richer pastures. Believe He is with you, receive His presence and enjoy it. Write down and keep close to you verses of Scripture that remind you of who God is like Hebrews 13:5 *"I will never leave thee, nor forsake thee."*

Each day I will commit to rest by:

_____

_____

Each week I will commit to rest by:

_____

_____

My preferred method of relaxation and Christian meditation is:

_____

_____

Depending on your preferred method list the visuals, images, or verses you will focus on during meditation:

_____

_____

Session 11 Group Exercise

1 Corinthians 6:19-20
Do you not know that your bodies are temples of the Holy Spirit, who is in you, whom you have received from God? You are not your own; you were bought at a price. Therefore honor God with your bodies

Mark 6:31
Come ye yourselves apart into a desert place, and rest a while.

Genesis 2:3
And God blessed the seventh day and made it holy, because on it he rested from all the work of creating that he had done.

Exodus 34:21
Six days you shall labor, but on the seventh day you shall rest; even during the plowing season and harvest you must rest.

Psalms 119:97
Oh how love I your law! It is my meditation all the day.
1:2
But his delight is in the law of the Lord, and on his law he meditates day and night.
48:9
Within your temple, O God, we meditate on your unfailing love.

Joshua 1:8
Do not let this Book of the Law depart from your mouth; meditate on it day and night, so that you may be careful to do everything written in it.

Exercise in Rest

Facilitator will lead the group by reading the following activity, dim the lights if possible, set a silent timer to go off in 25 minutes. Read to group in a soft, soothing tone of voice.

"Make yourself comfortable, uncross your legs, arms, remove shoes and glasses, lay flat on your back and close your eyes.

Clear your mind of worries or resentments. Claim peace and tranquility for yourself.

Raise your hands above your head and rest them, don't grasp anything. Take a deep breath, hold it for a few seconds, relax and breathe out.

Now stretch your hands up as far as they will go, farther, hold them there

Now push your feet down as far as they will go, farther, hold them there

Count slowly to 10 silently in your mind as I count to 10 aloud 1…2…3….4…5…6…7….8…9…10

Relax and let your hands and feet return to their original position

Count slowly to 10 silently in your mind as I count to 10 aloud 1…2…3….4…5…6…7….8…9…10

(repeat the stretch, count to 10, then repeat the relax, count to ten once more)

Breathe in and out slowly, rhythmically for a few minutes (4-5 minutes silently)

Remain immobile, resting and relaxing. Don't worry, I will mind the time

(When the timer goes off)

When you are ready, open your eyes, be aware of your body awakening, sit up slowly, moving slowly and peacefully, get up slowly"

Exercise in Christian Meditation- Self-Love

Facilitator will lead the group by reading the following activity, dim the lights if possible, set a silent timer to go off in 25 minutes and read the following in a soft, soothing tone of voice

Sit comfortably, remove shoes, glasses, rest your arms, hands palms up in your lap, close your eyes.

Breathe in and out, slowly, concentrating on listening to the sound of your breath

Relax and quiet your mind. Our mantra today will be *"God is love, I am love"* you may visualize the words or an image of God holding you in His arms.

Today we will set our intentions of finding and expanding self-love in our physical and energetic bodies

Consider who you are. Consider that God put you right where you are because he expresses his love only in very special ways

Visualize yourself and the joy and wonderment you have brought to others, your parents, your siblings, your children, friends, co-workers, even strangers. Invite them into your space and ask that they connect with you

Love what you have brought them

Appreciate how the special you was just what they needed in so many instances

Absorb the love they feel for you, visualize this love as God wrapping his arms around you and holding you firmly

Visualize that now you and God are one, God is love, I am love

Know now how it is that you came to be you in this time and place

Be still with that, it is perfection, it is pure, it is joy, it is love

People love you, people need you, people express love to you, you are a good person, forgive yourself for your mistakes. Mistakes are simply part of life, give them no emotion, definition or rationale, simply observe them and let them go away

Love yourself for experiencing mistakes

Visualize the joy and wonderment you have brought to God's creatures, love that sharing, hold it as a precious gift.

Be still with that, It is perfection, It is pure. It is joy.

Now silently focus on the mantra *"God is love, I am love"* release all thought except *God is love, I am love* repeating it over and over again.

Do not worry, I will mind the time, when it is time to release the mantra, you will hear the timer go off.

(Remain silent for the remainder of the session until the timer goes off)

(When the timer goes off)

It is time to release the mantra *"God is love, I am love.....God is love, I am love"* Thank you Lord for giving us this special time together.

When you are ready, slowly open your eyes, be aware of your body awakening, sit peacefully until you are ready to get up, get up slowly

RECOVER/DISCOVER

SESSION 12

Discover Your Godly Purpose

Discover Your Godly Purpose

God is not dwelling on our faults or failures and neither should we. God expects us to be His work-in-progress and he continually molds and shapes us into the characteristics that he wants us to adapt. Don't be discouraged about your past, trust that it develops you further onto greater things in store. While people may reject us, know that God loves us unconditionally and he will never reject us, therefore don't allow you to reject yourself.

When you are feeling that your circumstances are keeping you stuck in a rut, turn to David's inspiring recognition in Psalm 40 "*I waited patiently for the LORD, he turned to me and heard my cry, He lifted me out of the slimy pit, out of the mud and mire; He set my feet on a rock and gave me a firm place to stand. He put a new song in my mouth, a hymn of praise to our God. Many will see and fear and put their trust in the LORD.*" God will also put your feet upon a rock, and in time as his will for you unfolds, you also will be able to rejoice and praise the song he will put into your heart.

Many believe that it is only through this crisis, most difficult of times are we inspired to dig deep to discover ourselves and our true calling from God. All of our normal, daily distractions are removed at the height of our wounding and we are open to make sense out of the senselessness of our situation.

In *The Purpose Driven Life,* Rick Warren explains:

" We are not put on earth just to consume resources, but to make a permanent, significant contribution. We are created to serve God. The Bible says God has created us for a life of good deeds, which he has already prepared for us to do. When we serve others in any way (large or small) we are serving God and fulfilling our purposes. Not only were we created to serve, but we are *commanded* to serve. Matthew 20:28 "*Just as the Son of Man did not come to be served, but to serve, and to give his life as a ransom for many.*" For Christians service is not optional, something to squeeze in if the time allows, it is the heart of the Christian life. The mature follower stops asking "Who can serve me and meet my needs? and start asking "Whose needs can I meet?" At the end of our lives God will compare how much time and energy we spent on ourselves versus what we invested in serving others. Service is the pathway to real significance. God wants you to make a difference in his world. He wants to work through your crisis, your heartbreak, through YOUR experiences and give you your own pathway to serve others, love others. These experiences were not given to you for your own benefit, but for the benefit of others, just as others were given experiences that they will share for your benefit."

Many counselors will encourage one who is immobilized with sadness, depression or uncertainty to simply put their emotions aside and do something to help another, to volunteer to help someone or some organization that needs support. The benefits of this gesture are to temporarily take one's mindset off of themselves and dwelling in their present mode and focus on another's needs. This can be a very rewarding experience, something as simple as feeding a neighbor, driving a friend somewhere they need to go, stuffing envelopes for a non-profit organization. The distraction can be very therapeutic.

57

So, how do we discover how to serve? Warren gives us guidance:

"In determining your area for serving God, examine these six kinds of experiences from your past:

Family experiences: What did you learn growing up in your family?

Educational experiences: What were your favorite subjects in school?

Vocational experiences: What jobs have you been most effective in and enjoyed the most?

Spiritual experiences: What have been your most meaningful times with God?

Ministry experiences: How have you served God in the past that brought you joy?

Painful experiences: What problems, hurts, thorns and trials have you learned from?

It is the last category, painful experiences, that God uses the most to prepare you for ministry. God never wastes a hurt! In fact, your greatest ministry will most likely come out of your greatest hurt. He intentionally lets you go through painful experiences to equip you for your service.

2 Corinthians 1:3 *"Praise be to the God and Father of our Lord Jesus Christ, the Father of compassion and God of all comfort, who comforts us in our troubles so that we can comfort others. When others are troubled, we will be able to give them the same comfort God has given us."*

The very experiences you have resented or regretted the most are the ones you have been given to be used to help others! For God to use your experiences, you must be willing to share them. People are always more encouraged when we share how God's grace helped us in our weakest times rather than brag about our strengths. Experience is not what happens to you, it is what you do with that experience that is the key. Don't waste your pain, use it to help others."

Session 12 Group Exercise

Proverbs 19:21

Many are the plans in a person's heart, but it is the LORD's purpose that prevails

Encouraging quotes from God Calling

p. 232 Give, give, give all your best to all who need it. Be great givers. Give as I said My Father in Heaven gives. Pray to become great givers.

p. 246 Be not afraid, health and wealth are coming to you both. My wealth which is sufficiency for your needs, and for my work you long to do.

p.247 Never lose sight of the glorious work to which you have been called.

Paraphrasing a discussion between Talk Show Host, Oprah Winfrey and Rick Warren, Author of *A Purpose Driven Life*:

*The best use of life is love, the best expression of love is time, the best time to love is now. You will find your purpose and your purpose will become significant when you serve others. That's how you raise yourself from acknowledging your purpose and current success to a **significant** life that creates a legacy.*

What experience can I offer to use to serve others?

_____

_____

_____

_____

Identify your likes and dislikes. What are you passionate about? Figure out what you love to do-what God gave you a heart to do, and then do it for his glory.

What are my likes, passions, what do I love to do?

_____

_____

_____

In the next Session we will help devise a plan to merge the two (experiences and likes) to help you find your purpose and put a plan into place that will give you a significant opportunity to make a difference in your life and others.

RECOVER/DISCOVER

SESSION 13

Live Your Godly Purpose

Live Your Godly Purpose

In _The Purpose Driven Life_, Rick Warren gives clear ways to figure out where your purpose to serve will ultimately become clear. He explains that the best way to discover your gifts is to try experimenting with different ways to serve. Don't wait to volunteer until you define your gifts, throw yourself into a variety of ways to serve others and your gifts and talents will emerge when you begin to feel passion about one area or another. Until you start serving, you're not going to know what you are good at. Some ideas he suggests are:

1) Try teaching, leading or organizing for a program or entity
2) Play an instrument or sing
3) Work with teenagers in youth groups, tutoring or mentoring in Big Brother or YMCA or YWCA programs
4) Volunteer free time to a non-profit organization, hospital or elder care facility
5) Serve at a local Food Bank, Homeless Sheltor or Soup Kitchen, or Domestic Violence Advocacy
6) Volunteer in your neighborhood to coordinate or coach youth sports programs
7) Organize or volunteer for a fundraising event for a well-deserving charity
8) Find a group who has similar painful experiences and share your story and testimony

And share your testimony along the way, those who are suffering need your testimony to understand and develop hope for healing. Include the following points when you share your life experiences to help others grow and heal:

What has God taught me from failure or heartache?
What has God taught me from lack of money or resources?
What has God taught me from pain, sorrow or depression?
What has God taught me through waiting?
What has God taught me through illness?
What has God taught me from disappointment?
What have I learned from my family, my church, my relationships, my small group?

Be patient with yourself as you try new areas of service. If one area just isn't right for you, try another. When it doesn't work out, don't consider it a failure, consider it an experiment, you will eventually learn what you are good at. You will find that people who don't understand your desire to find and perfect your gift will criticize you and try to get you to conform to what they think you should be doing, but _ignore them!_

Once you have determined your gift and area of service, remember to have the authentic intention to serve. Having the heart of a true servant to God means serving without expectation of personal gain, being available to serve when the need arises, always looking for those in need and someone to serve, and simply doing what needs to be done.

Some of God's most glorious opportunities to serve come in the smallest, most discreet of packages. A true servant doesn't need recognition or notoriety for their efforts. Jesus reminds us of this in Matthew 6 *"Be careful not to do your acts of righteousness before men, to be seen by them. If you do, you will have no reward from your Father in heaven. So when you give to the needy, do not announce it with trumpets, as the hypocrites do in the synagogues and on the streets, to be honored by men. I tell you the truth, they have received their reward in full. But when you give to the needy, do not let your left hand know what your right hand is doing, so that your giving may be in secret. Then your Father who sees what is done in secret will reward you.*

The most significant service is often the service that is unseen. Unseen by man, but God sees everything.

So ask yourself, who do I desire to help the most? And get to it!

Which of the above Serving suggestions appeals to me the most? (list in priority of interest)
1)_____
2_____
3)_____
4)_____

When wrapping up the final session of the group, establish an "Accountability follow-up". One month after the last session, circulate an email to the group participants having them report to all what action(s) they have taken to begin to identify their purpose.

Session 13 Group Exercise

Sharing our testimony can be painful but can be most healing when taken from the perspective of how God wants us to use it for his good. Take a moment to consider your experiences and journal below your interpretation of what this taught you through the growth of your faith. Those courageous enough can share their testimony with the group.

My experience(s) in bullet points:

* _____
* _____
* _____
* _____
* _____
* _____
* _____

Based on these experiences I believe God taught me:

God taught me from (failure or heartache)
_____

God taught me from (lack of money or resources)
_____

God taught me from (pain, sorrow or depression)
_____

God taught me through waiting:
_____

God taught me through (illness):
_____

God taught me from disappointment:
_____

God taught me from (fill in your own word) _____:
_____

God taught me from (fill in your own word) _____:
_____

What have I learned from my family, my church, my relationships, my small group?
_____
_____

RESOURCES

Citations and Suggested Additional Readings:

Creative Visualization – Shakti Gawain

Deceived - Claudia Black

Making Good Habits – Joyce Meyer

Peace From Broken Pieces - Iyanla Vanzant

The Anxiety Cure - Dr. Archibald D. Hart

The Purpose Driven Life - Rick Warren

Additional Inspirational Readings:

The Four Agreements - Don Miguel Ruiz

God Calling - A.J. Russell

Jesus Calling - Sarah Young

The Prayer of Jabez – Bruce Wilkinson

You Can Heal Your Life - Louise L. Hay

Forgiving Forward: Unleashing the Forgiveness Revolution – Bruce /Toni Hebel

www.ingramcontent.com/pod-product-compliance
Lightning Source LLC
Chambersburg PA
CBHW081157090426
42736CB00017B/3368

* 9 7 8 0 9 8 9 2 9 1 6 1 3 *